A DELIGHTFUL MESS OF CONTRADICTIONS

Natalie Veper

BookLeaf Publishing

India | USA | UK

Presentation by *BookLeaf Publishing*

Web: www.bookleafpub.com

E-mail: info@bookleafpub.com

ISBN: 9789358361391

First edition 2021

HEALING

it has always struck me

as quite odd

how uncomfortable

and unusual healing is

everyone tells you

how well you are doing

how much happier you look

how you are glowing

but what they don't seem to notice

are the raw pieces

of flesh

that you have scrubbed away

that have just been exposed

to air

and how much they itch

ADULTING

do more

do less

relax

feel guilty

you inadequate overachiever

focus on your sleep

we all have the same amount of hours in the day

get up early

stay up late

read this

listen to that

have you watched this yet?

call your friends

call your mum

call your nan

compare yourself to everyone online

switch off your phone

swipe left, swipe right

be careful not to super like

stop scrolling

relax!

didn't I tell you to relax?

why aren't you relaxing already?

SLEEP

when

did it become so elusive?

why

is there suddenly

so much pressure

on doing something

that should be effortless?

is it because

your racing thoughts

terrify you

at 3am?

and for some reason

they don't have as

much power

when the sun streams through your window again?

BOSTON

it flashes

and you scramble to answer

although

you don't really need to

you already know what she is going

to say

he is gone

and you think you are okay

after all

he was only a dog

but you wail

and gasp for air

because little do

they know

that little dog

is the reason you are still here

DROWNING

torn between

being bored

feeling stagnant

yet wanting to do more

or learn something new

while drowning in responsibilities

and commitments

JEANS

we all have

that one pair

hiding in the back of our cupboard

you haven't worn them in years

in fact

they probably no longer fit

you've outgrown them

you've changed your style

and you're trying to grow

and they don't really make you feel the same way anymore

so why can't you let them go?

THE RULES

surely by now

you've realised

that you feel

your absolute worst

when you start

trying to play

the game

by someone else's rules

you fucking hate rules?

FITTING IN

I always

struggle when I see people

upset about not fitting in

maybe it is because

you've owned your

weird, but bad arse self

since you were 16

and you are

pretty okay

with swimming upstream

rather than going with the flow

you just have to find your people

no, not those ones

WINTER

there will always be something magical

about the smell

of those first cold nights

that will always remind you

of your childhood

and running around

playing in the dark

watching your breath

as you exhaled

MONDAY MORNING

she always struts on in

without warning

the click clack

of her cheap heels

jolt you

from your fitful and interrupted sleep

and then she reprimands you

for how much time

you wasted over the last two days

WANDERING AND WONDERING

why is it that you can be

fully aware

that the shit

swirling through your head

isn't real

but you still allow it

to have so much power

over how you feel?

WHEN?

and I often

ask myself

when will we know?

when will we know that we have made it?

THE RAT RACE

just remember

even if

you are ahead of the pack

spinning

the fastest on the wheel

you are

still

just

a

fucking rat

FTP

I am so very

fucking sorry

for not speaking up

to support you

when the men were mocking women

but I am still

trying to figure out

whether I'm tuning out

because I am not ready

to be reminded

of what I escaped

or whether I am resisting the urge

to implode

or explode

instead

I am trying to remain calm

and unbothered

because

there is nothing they want more

than an

emotional response

from another

hysterical

woman

NOT YOURS

you think

that you know

everything about me

but really,

you don't know who

you are dealing with at all

SWIRLING

my head is swirling again

and I'm so tired of being tired

what a rollercoaster

these surges

and drops

often provide

GUILT

I feel

like I shouldn't

speak up

about what you consider

to be

all of this petty shit

but I remember

there are people

who need to hear

it doesn't only

happen to them

and that it shouldn't be us

made to feel like the minority

THE QUIETEST OF TEARS

I feel like

I've been crying in my sleep again

waking up

double breathing

always exposes me

it must be

the only time

I allow myself

to feel

FADING FACADE

how can it be

that you spend

your whole life

feeling

completely misunderstood

then you find

one or two

people that

see through your facade

it drives you wild

because they see you

exactly

for who you are?

GROWTH

we are encouraged

to aspire

for growth

as it appears

life will be far...simpler?

but I am still waiting

to be warned about

the amount of mourning

in walking away

from people

who won't even notice

you

are

gone